BOOKWORMS

The Inside Story
Castle

Dana Meachen Rau

Marshall Cavendish
Benchmark
New York

Inside a Castle

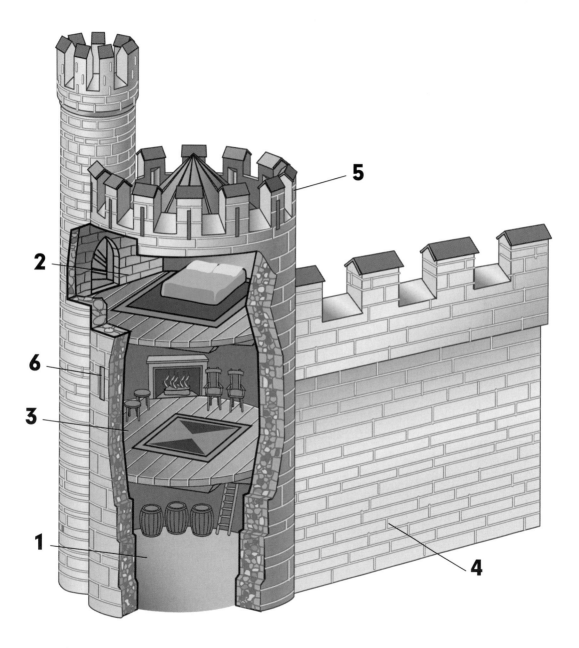

Castles are very old.

They are made of stone.

Lords lived in castles.

Castles kept them safe.

Castles had strong walls.

They had tall towers.

A *moat* went around
the castle.

A *drawbridge* crossed
the water.

People went in through a gatehouse.

It had strong wooden doors and a metal gate.

Towers had three or four rooms inside.

Stairs led to each one.

The basement was on
the bottom.

A meeting room was in
the middle.

The top room was a bedroom.

Fireplaces kept the rooms warm.

The castle had a *chapel*.

People prayed in it.

The castle had a big hall.

People had parties in the hall.

The castle had a jail.

The jail was under a door in the floor.

Many people worked in
the castle.

They kept the lord happy
and safe.

Inside a Castle

gatehouse

jail

moat

stairs

tower

Challenge Words

chapel (CHAP-uhl) A room or building for praying.

drawbridge (DRAW-brij) A wooden bridge that could be raised or lowered.

lords Important people who served a king.

moat (MOHT) The water around a castle.

29

Index

Page numbers in **boldface** are illustrations.

About the Author

Dana Meachen Rau is an author, editor, and illustrator. A graduate of Trinity College in Hartford, Connecticut, she has written more than one hundred fifty books for children, including nonfiction, biographies, early readers, and historical fiction. She lives with her family in Burlington, Connecticut.

Reading Consultants

Nanci Vargus, Ed.D. is an Assistant Professor of Elementary Education at the University of Indianapolis.

Beth Walker Gambro received her M.S. Ed. Reading from the University of St. Francis, Joliet, Illinois.

With thanks to Nanci Vargus, Ed.D. and
Beth Walker Gambro, reading consultants

Marshall Cavendish Benchmark
Marshall Cavendish
99 White Plains Road
Tarrytown, New York 10591-9001
www.marshallcavendish.us

Library of Congress Cataloging-in-Publication Data

Rau, Dana Meachen, 1971–
Castle / by Dana Meachen Rau.
p. cm. — (Bookworms. The inside story)
Summary: "Descibes the architecture, construction,
and interior of a castle"—Provided by publisher.
Includes index.
ISBN-13: 978-0-7614-2272-3
ISBN-10: 0-7614-2272-2
1. Castles—Juvenile literature. I. Title. II. Series.
NA7710.R34 2006
728.8'1—dc22
2005029852

Photo Research by Anne Burns Images

Cover Photo by Corbis/G.Rossenbach/zefa

The photographs in this book are used with permission and through the courtesy of:
Corbis: pp. 1, 11, 28b Peter Adams/zefa; p. 5 Michael Busselle; pp. 9, 29tr Royalty Free;
pp. 15, 29tl Sandro Vannini; p. 21 Michael St. Maur Shell; p. 23 Richard T. Nowitz;
p. 27 Historical Picture Archive. Art Resource: pp. 7, 13, 19, 25, 28tl, 28tr Erich Lessing.
Image Works: p. 17 National Trust Photo Library/James Mortimer.

Printed in Malaysia
1 3 5 6 4 2